T0193617

Understanding
Your
Identity

Understanding Your Identity

PHILIP OLUWASANYA

WESTBOW
PRESS®
A DIVISION OF THOMAS NELSON
& ZONDERVAN

WestBow Press books may be ordered through booksellers or by contacting:

WestBow Press
A Division of Thomas Nelson & Zondervan
1663 Liberty Drive
Bloomington, IN 47403
www.westbowpress.com
1 (866) 928-1240

Scripture taken from the King James Version of the Bible.

This book is a work of non-fiction. Unless otherwise noted, the author and the publisher make no explicit guarantees as to the accuracy of the information contained in this book and in some cases, names of people and places have been altered to protect their privacy.

ISBN: 978-1-9736-1533-0 (sc)
ISBN: 978-1-9736-1532-3 (e)

Library of Congress Control Number: 2018900539

Print information available on the last page.

WestBow Press rev. date: 1/29/2018

To God Almighty for the opportunity, ability, and grace to write and be a channel of His Word to the world.

I give to Him first—that He may give me the rest and the best.

To God be the glory!

ACKNOWLEDGMENTS

I acknowledge my family for their patience and understanding for the days I am in a sort of reverie, as I brood over my thoughts and contents of this book, and when I just stay away from everything and do seem not to have time for them. Thank you for your understanding.

I appreciate Pastor Tokunboh Adejuwon (deputy national director, Rhema, Nigeria) and Pastor Gbenga Ogunyemi (Reigning Kings International Ministries) for their valuable comments after reviewing the initial concepts and contents of this book.

Finally, thank you to Dr. Kenneth Otah for your encouragement and physical and moral support to take the step to finally publish this book.

God bless you all.

CONTENTS

CHAPTER 1

Who Are You?

After finishing a program at the Bible college, I was full of glee and enthusiasm about spreading my experience and newfound insights on God's Word to everyone and anyone willing to listen. I believed I was having a wonderful time with the Lord. He opened my eyes to new things in the scriptures. I was beginning to feel high with myself, feeling that I had arrived. I did not realize that the Lord was revealing my relationship with Him to me.

There have been times when I've really messed up and derailed myself. I have done things I would never have believed I could get myself into. However, in recent times, I have had the confidence to conquer myself enough to say I have a clean slate with the Lord. To top it all off, I went to Bible college because I felt led by the Lord to do so. The experience—during and after the program—was quite heavenly.

During the final months of the program, I had a swell time in the presence of the Lord. I had never felt that way before. I was able to write a sermon every time I opened the Bible. It was amazing. Even a search for a particular scripture to support or clarify a biblical issue gave rise to another revelation.

Then, I had a dream.

In the dream, I found myself sitting on a high concrete cauldron inside a compound. The cauldron was shaped like a trapezoid and was about five feet high. As I sat within the compound, I was informed that a former Bible college classmate would have to pass through my compound to get to where he was going.

As he approached, I said, "My pastor, my pastor." That was the way we students normally called each other in class. However, he did not respond the way I expected. He was sort of miffed over something, and he didn't waste any time letting me know what was eating him up. He expressed his displeasure and disappointment that people on my street were so undisciplined and uncultured. They were defecating on the streets and littering the gutters with excrement. The disgust on his face was quite dramatic.

I tried to calm him down with my words. I told him that people were useless, undisciplined, and inconsiderate of other road users, but it did not have any effect. I decided to get down from where I was sitting, get close to him, and talk with him more; I would castigate whoever had defecated in the street.

Due to the height of the cauldron, it had to tilt so I could step down. I didn't know the cauldron contained anything. In fact, it was actually a septic tank that contained the sewage of people in my compound. Tilting the cauldron caused the sewage to spill out onto my shorts. From the expression on my friend's face, I could tell it was worse than what he had been complaining about in the first place.

I reeked so much that I was ashamed of myself. I was sitting on the high cauldron like a leader in the compound, but I was the object of ridicule due to the stench covering my body. It was such a depressing situation, and I wished the ground would open so I could disappear.

As I was standing there in my shame, I heard a little voice speaking to me. It said, "Do you see how easy it is to talk down to people when you are actually doing the same —if not worse—as them? You joined your friend to complain about the ills of others—just to make your friend happy. All the while, you were sitting on a cauldron of sewage that was meant to be buried underground until it spilled on you and exposed your own filth and that you had been hiding under a presumed throne. When others saw you, they considered you an upright person. They did not know that you were enthroned on filth. This is what I have been teaching you over the past months. Do you recall the topic you used for your Bible college project ("Identity Crisis: The Nemesis of Creation")? You need to have proper insight into who you are in every period of your life. To you, it is a revelation to teach to others, excluding yourself. Do you not know that every lesson you will be required to teach the body of Christ starts with you?"

"God's word is as a double-edged sword" (Hebrews 4:12). These words were so profound and very disquieting, and they were all true and on point.

When I woke up and thought about it, I followed the trail of events in the past seven or eight months. The Lord had been taking me on a different schooling experience besides from my Bible college sojourn. The Lord started with my Bible college dissertation and was moving me to other areas of my life. I lost considerable kingdom assets to the devil by allowing him to cloud my mind due to my ignorance of my true identity—as a human being and as a believer in Jesus Christ.

I would like to share some of the insights the Lord has brought to my attention. I strongly believe they will be of immense value to you and the body of Christ as we look to understand our identities in the Lord Jesus.

I would like to start with some definitions of identity and how identity relates to us as human beings.

Identity

A person's identity signifies his or her individuality, which differentiates one person from another apart from gender (male and female). Each gender has its own individuality. Your identity talks about your character, your personality, and what makes you who you are.

According to the *Oxford Dictionary*, identity is who or what something is; the characteristics, feelings, or beliefs that distinguish people from others.

Identity can be manifested and understood under three broad headings: who, what, and why.

Who: This explains your personality as far as your behaviors, traits, and characteristics, how you will react to things, and how situations or circumstances affect you.

What: This explains your content or substance. Are you a living thing? Are you an animal or a human? Are you male or female?

Why: This looks at your purpose or responsibility, the reason you are what or where you are, the functions that you have to undertake at a specific time and place, and a job or duty that you are saddled with at any given time, place, or occasion.

Factors Affecting Identity

One's identity can be determined by factors like environment, situations, or circumstances. The environment where individuals find themselves will affect their identities. Imagine, for instance, that you are the managing director of the world's biggest organization and have been invited to a function where presidents of nations are present. Your identity will command some respect. However, it will still be subject to the dictates of the protocol officers of the various heads of states. You will not go to the high table and order people around or have them cowering at your presence. In such an environment, your identity does not command such powers as it does when you are in your office or around your subordinates.

Imagine if you were the head of a nation, but when you go home to your parents and elder siblings, your identity is that of their child and younger sibling. It matters not that you can make decisions that affect their lives as well as others on a daily basis. When you are with them, you will take orders from them and obey them on issues that regard the family.

In a similar way, situations and circumstances can affect an individual's identity at a given time or place. For instance, a typical law-abiding citizen of a country might be wrongfully accused of a crime that he or she did not commit, which is common in Nigeria. Where the police indiscriminately arrest people for wandering, putting them in jail, or even accuse them of one crime or another to cover up for the police's lapses, the individual loses his or her identity of being a law-abiding citizen and becomes an accused or an enemy of the state, depending on the alleged crime.

The circumstances of a loss or gain can also affect the identity of an individual. In the event of a positive gain, such as giving birth, getting married, or building a house, the individual becomes a mother or father from being childless, a husband or wife from being a bachelor or a spinster, or a homeowner from being a tenant. In negative circumstances, the loss of one's spouse transforms a married individual into a widow or widower, the loss of a job to being jobless, the loss of accommodations to being homeless, and so on.

Effects of Identity

One's identity can have a positive or negative effect on the individual. Your identity either adds to you or takes away from you.

Your identity determines how people relate with you and sometimes how you relate to others. You will either be in control or be the controlled. For instance, a helper cannot control the master unless the master has committed an infraction. If the situation affects the identity of the master, the helper is now in control. For example, a leader who sexually harasses a subordinate in the office or institutes an illicit relationship with a subordinate will lose his or her identity as a leader to such a subordinate. The former leader will be under the control of that subordinate since the liaison is illicit and needs to be kept a secret. The subordinate can control the leader by blackmailing the leader.

This brings up several questions. What are our identities in Christ? Are we servants? Are we slaves? Some religions profess that you can be nothing more than a slave or a servant to God, the Creator of heaven and the earth. That is contrary to what the Bible tells us even from the beginning of creation. Genesis 1:26 states that we were created in His image to have dominion. Our shared identity is our first qualification on earth. We are created in His image!

CHAPTER 2

His Image

And God said; Let us make man in our image, after
our likeness: and let them have dominion over the
fish of the sea, and over the birds of the heavens,
and over the cattle, and over all the earth, and over
every creeping thing that creepeth upon the earth.
—Genesis 1:26

Our first identity is found in our creation. The book
of our beginning, Genesis, records that, when God
created us, He said, "Let us make man in our image, after
our likeness."

So, what we are? We are made in the image and likeness of
God, and as we all know, if we are created thus, we can only
be one thing: gods. The one who made plants and animals
to replicate after their kind will not create something in His
own image and likeness only for that thing to be something
less than God Himself.

Doth the fountain send forth from the same
opening sweet water and bitter?
Can a fig tree, my brethren, yield olives, or a
vine, figs? Neither can salt water yield sweet.
(James 3:11–12)

James elaborated on the fact that everything will reproduce and replicate after its kind, and that is exactly what God did by creating us in His own image, after His likeness. That is why He directed us to have dominion over all His other creations.

We represent God here on earth, and He also affirmed it when He declared, "Ye are gods" (Psalm 82). That same verse continues that we are all children of the Most High, which fits into the what and who of our identities.

If we all agree that we are gods who are to have dominion over all of God's creations with no exception, can we sincerely say that we are occupying this position and exhibiting the traits of one in dominion? The answer is yes and no.

That may look like a contradiction, but those are the available facts. We have been able to have control of creation to an extent. Results abound of humans' exploits in taming and training animals, harnessing the medicinal and other benefits of plants, and so on. However, in all of these, we still face challenges when we see animals turning on their trainers and harming or killing them. We have also suffered due to errors in the harnessing of substances from plants, which sometimes has deadly consequences.

Humans have not been able to achieve 100 percent

compliance with the mandate issued to us in the beginning, and this is not unconnected to the incident that occurred in the garden of Eden. That brought about a great debacle for humans, losing the position of dominion to the devil, who outsmarted man.

The fall of Adam and Eve in the garden of Eden was actually an understanding issue. We lost the value of our identities and failed to grasp the value of our identities, thereby handing over our position of dominion on earth to the devil through an act of disobedience. A quick look at that event shows how the devil cunningly twisted human understanding in the garden of Eden.

> Now the serpent was more subtle than any beast of the field, which the Lord God had made. And he said unto the woman, Yea, hath God said, Ye shall not eat of every tree of the garden?
> And the woman said unto the serpent, We may eat of the fruit of the trees of the garden:
> But of the fruit of the tree which is in the midst of the garden, God hath said, Ye shall not eat of it, neither shall ye touch it, lest ye die.
> And the serpent said unto the woman, Ye shall not surely die:
> For God doth know that in the day ye eat thereof, then your eyes shall be opened, and ye shall be as gods, knowing good and evil.
> And when the woman saw that the tree was good for food, and that it was pleasant to the eyes, and a tree to be desired to make one wise, she took of the fruit thereof, and did eat, and gave also unto her husband with her; and he did eat. (Genesis 3:1–6)

Our main focus in this story is when the devil—through the serpent—stated, "If they eat of the specific fruit, it will make them be like God."

Genesis 1 states that we were created in the image and likeness of God—and not in the image of any other thing. If something was produced in the image of a specific object, it will always be like that very object. If a new basket is made in the image of an existing basket, the new one will surely be like the old basket. Therefore, when God made us in His image and likeness, we were already like God. But in the passage in focus (Genesis 3:5) the serpent said that when humans eat of the fruit that we will then be like God. In reality, we were already like God because we were created in the image and likeness of God in the first place.

When one lacks the understanding of something, misuse and abuse is inevitable. That can be catastrophic—just like in this case.

Let us look at what humanity lost because of that act of disobedience. Adam and Eve lacked a thorough understanding of their identities. Genesis 1–2 will give us some insights.

God's Image

Humans, in the image of God, shared some qualities with God: immortality, knowledge, and glory. After the Fall, Adam and Eve lost their covering of glory, which was why the first thing they noticed was their nakedness. God had to provide them with coverings of animal skin.

The loss of this glory is the reason why animals that hitherto were obedient to humans will now attack us when they feel threatened.

Every time we disobey God, we lose our covering. We become susceptible to attacks and the wiles of the devil. He can easily harm us or attempt to. A case in point is the story of a young prophet who was given an express instruction not to stay back or eat in the city he was sent to. An older prophet deceived him, and he ended up being eaten by an animal on his way back home (1 Kings 13). This didn't happen to him on his way to his assignment; it was not recoded that he encountered an animal on that leg of his journey; however, as soon as he disobeyed, he lost his covering and his life.

Humans lost their immortality and became mere mortals. It is recorded that nobody lived a complete day in the sight of God. "A thousand years is as a day before God" (2 Peter 3:8). The man who lived the longest was Methuselah, and he lived for 969 years.

This phenomenon of people not living long lives became more common as evil grew due to their constant acts of disobedience to God and His instructions. If God had not come in again to peg the age man was to live to seventy years and by reason of strength eighty years (Psalm 90:10), who knows if man will live up to forty years because of the effect of disobedience and sin.

Dominion

When humankind fell, we lost our authority. We lost what gave us rulership over creation. The Bible makes us understand that God created us and gave us the mandate to have dominion over all He created.

The moment Adam disobeyed, we lost the ability to fulfill that mandate. His disobedience resulted in God declaring the consequences of his action, which were curses upon all the actors in the disobedience.

Enmity between Humans and Animals

The first curse was to the animal that the devil used in deceiving humans. The snake lost its form, and God set enmity between it and humankind that it would henceforth bruise the heels of men and women, in the same way humans would bruise its head (Genesis 3:14–15).

That was the same animal that came to Eve in the beginning without fear or fight. They had a discussion on the instructions of God concerning the fruits in the garden, which then led to the debacle. The animal became cursed. The fact that they talked could only mean there was no hostility between them before the curse that God laid upon them. Humankind lost its position of authority and would have to be afraid of the snake from then on.

Ease of Life

Humanity lost the privilege of achieving things with ease. People were in charge, and they were meant to live life with a lot of ease. Eve got the first blow. She was to have pain and henceforth give birth in pain (Genesis 3:16). God decreed that her pains would be greatly increased. It is no surprise that women are faced with various challenges today. Some live as single parents and fend for their families. Before the Fall, everything was done with ease by virtue of her position as someone in dominion.

Adam was hit most. The curse affects people's everyday lives and their livelihoods. Humans have to toil to eat. Before the Fall, Adam had no need to till the ground to get food. Everything he needed was already in the garden. All he needed to do was manage what was provided and not start food production from scratch.

Farming must have been incredibly tedious in those days with the sort of crude implements that would have been available to Adam.

His Home

Adam and Eve lost their first home due to disobedience. They became wanderers because God had to chase them out of the home He made for them. From grace to grass, humanity lost its dominion of being a homeowner and ended up as wanderers.

People without roofs over their heads are not in control of anything. They are subject to environmental elements, laws, and hazards.

Knowledge

After God created Adam, He acknowledged that it was not ideal for him to be alone. In the process of finding Adam a suitable companion, He brought all the animals He had created to Adam, hoping that they would be his companion. Alas, none was found of them all (Genesis 2:18–20). The remarkable thing in this passage is the fact that Adam was so knowledgeable that he gave names to all the animals, and those are the names we call them today.

In addition, I want to believe that Adam's memory would have been so acute that he could remember each animal's name.

Why do we still have to name animals today when Adam already named them. How come we find it hard to remember things now the way Adam was able to remember the names of all the animals. The answer is found in the Fall at the garden of Eden. Humans lost their strength of knowledge—even though the Bible recorded that they had the knowledge of good and evil. People lost the knowledge of being in control of all they surveyed. Adam was able to name the animals and remember them.

The Fall was devastating for Adam. He lost very important

traits and benefits because he lacked understanding about his true identity.

The good news is that it does not have to remain that way. Adam lost his identity due to sin, disobedience, and a lack of understanding. The price for that negligence has been paid. Our true identities have been ransomed and restored. All that is needed is to understand what price was paid, how it was paid for, and what new privileges we have in our new identities.

CHAPTER 3

Paid For

For ye are bought with a price: therefore glorify God
in your body, and in your spirit, which are God's.
—1 Corinthians 6:20

When Adam disobeyed and lost his position in the garden, he lost his identity to be like God, which was contrary to what the devil wanted him to believe. Adam became a mere mortal, losing all the benefits of his identity as the man in charge of the earth. He no longer had dominion over all of God's creations.

Adam became a homeless wanderer. He had to fend for himself. He had to survive, learn how to live on earth, and relate to God. The effect of his disobedience was immediately evident in the lives of his children. Cain killed his brother, and sin became a way of life. It is recorded in the Bible that acts of sin increased progressively.

God is very concerned about us because He does not see Himself only as a Creator. He is also our Father, and He loves us with an everlasting love. He went ahead and made amends for our lives by paying the price for our sins.

Adam and Eve sinned, but God paid the price. The price for sin is death—the shedding of blood.

> For when Moses had spoken every precept to all the people according to the law, he took the blood of calves and of goats, with water, and scarlet wool, and hyssop, and sprinkled both the book, and all the people,
> Saying, This is the blood of the testament which God hath enjoined unto you.
> Moreover he sprinkled with blood both the tabernacle, and all the vessels of the ministry.
> And almost all things are by the law purged with blood; and without shedding of blood is no remission. (Hebrews 9:19–22)

Blood needs to be shed for sins to be covered or for the consequences of sin to be reduced or abated. In the scripture above, Moses is said to sprinkle the blood of the animal that was used to stand in the place of the children of Israel. They acknowledged their sins as a people and on the altar to signify their blood being shed. They offered it as a price for their sins.

That act was carried out annually as a sign of submission and realization that humans have sinned. Since shedding the blood of man will invariably mean the death of all men on earth, God gave the privilege of using the blood of animal. An animal cannot truly represent man since its blood cannot take the place of human blood (Hebrews 10:1–4).

The real offenders have to pay for what they have done. We have a responsibility to pay for our acts of rebellion and disobedience. That is where our loving heavenly Father went the extra mile on our behalf. He paid the price for the last time. He bought us with the price of blood—as stipulated by the law of remission. He paid with the price of his Son, Jesus Christ.

We were created in the image and likeness of God, which makes us gods. For the sin of a god to be remitted, the blood of a god is required. God—in showing His love for us and being willing to pay the price for our sins—had to pay with the blood of a god since we were no longer in His image.

God went a step further by giving the blood of His Son. God that cannot lose His image, and He cannot forget or lose appreciation for His true identity—unlike man.

> For God so loved the world, that he gave his only begotten Son, that whosoever believeth in him should not perish, but have everlasting life. (John 3:16)

Jesus came and decided to make Himself like what man had become so that He could feel and relate with us the way we currently are—in our fallen, mortal state. That way, there could be no argument that Jesus could go through what He had to go through in order to truly and fully represent us since His own blood would be shed for us.

> Let this mind be in you, which was also in Christ Jesus:

Who, being in the form of God, thought it not robbery to be equal with God:
But made himself of no reputation, and took upon him the form of a servant, and was made in the likeness of men: And being found in fashion as a man, he humbled himself, and became obedient unto death, even the death of the cross. (Philippians 2:5–8)

Jesus also relinquished His true identity as a Supreme God, His position in heaven, His immortality, and the attendant glory to take on the form of a mortal man. He went through tempting dialogue that Eve went through with the same devil. In His case, He was very aware of His identity—irrespective of His environment or circumstance.

If you do not know who you are, compromise is inevitable. It was recorded that the devil visited Jesus in the same way he visited Eve. This time, it was not in a relaxed atmosphere of a garden, but in a dusty desert. To add insult to injury, Jesus was hungry since He had been fasting for forty days and nights.

It is scientifically proven that humans can live without food for up to eight days, but we can only live without water for five days. Jesus had not had food for forty days, and He was offered a bread buffet. Just speaking the word would turn stones to bread. Jesus is the Word of God, and all things were created by Him (John 1:1–3).

If Jesus had turned the stone to bread, it would mean that He was not really sure who or what He was (God). That would have been trying to prove what he was made of and capable of doing to the devil and the world. It was not the place for a King to prove to His subject that He had authority because He was the authority. This was also true for the two other requests from the devil ("Jump and you will be caught," "Bow to me, and I will give you all the kingdoms").

Jesus fully appreciated His identity as the Creator who was in charge of all the angels in heaven. As the owner of all kingdoms, He stood His ground. He did not allow the devil to trick Him into proving what He already was. Jesus reminded the devil that everything had already been provided for by God:

1. Man shall not live by bread alone.
2. Thou shall not tempt the Lord thy God.
3. Get thee behind me, Satan (simply: get lost).

Jesus came and took the place of humans. Just as the blood of animals was used to represent the blood of humankind to remit for our sins, Jesus finally went to the cross for humanity and shed His own blood to pay the ultimate price for sin once and for all (Hebrews 9:28). This act opened another way for us to be reconciled to God and get back the identity we lost in the garden of Eden.

For man to regain his identity through the price paid by Jesus for man's sins, it only requires man to believe in Jesus, what He has done and accept it for himself: man will immediately change identity from being a mere man, to become the son of God. (John 1:12)

We have regained an identity as beings created in the image and likeness of God. We are identified as sons and daughters of God, begotten of God Himself. The act of Jesus changed us from small gods into the big God. God—who created the various plants and animals and commanded that they should reproduce after their kind—would not give birth to a Son who was not like Him or even Him.

CHAPTER 4

Adopted

To redeem them that were under the law, that
we might receive the adoption of sons.
—Galatians 4:5

How can this be, how can a full-grown man
be reborn from the mother's womb?
—John 3:4

The answer is adoption. The price paid by Jesus was like
the processing fee that is charged to adopt a child or
adopt a pet. Once the adoption process has been completed,
the child belongs to you. There might be a change of name,
and a certificate will state that the child is now yours.

The work of redemption by Jesus—coming as a man,
living on earth like a man, suffering shame and reproach
like a man, and finally shedding His blood on the cross at
Calvary—was the adoption process. Since Adam lost his

identity in the garden of Eden, God did not want humankind to be destroyed. He subjected us to rules and regulations, hoping that we would abide by them. However, the Bible affirms that our hearts are desperately wicked. Abiding by those laws was not possible, and that warranted the outright buying over of humankind.

Jesus Christ was transformed into a lamb, similar to the ones been slaughtered by Moses and the priests of old for the remission of sins. Just as the sin of humankind was being transferred to the animal to be sacrificed by the priest, God transformed Jesus to take our place. "He was made sin who knew no sin" (2 Corinthians 5:21).

Our adoption is far beyond the physical human adoption I mentioned. It was a total transformation. Jesus was transformed into the animal for sacrifice. We were transformed from men and women into the sons and daughters of God—while receiving new spirits.

> For ye have not received the spirit of bondage again to fear; but ye have received the Spirit of adoption, whereby we cry, Abba, Father. (Romans 8:15)

We receive the Spirit, and it changes who we are. We become new people.

When God created us, He created us in His image and likeness. We were God's toys, and just like a toy maker, He made us look like Him. After the Fall, we became mortals—without authority—and we lost our resemblance to God.

God paid the price for our sin with the blood of His Son. We did not return to the likeness of God. We were transformed into new beings. We were given new spirits when we accepted what Jesus did on our behalf.

> Therefore, if any man be in Christ, he is a new creature: old things are passed away; behold, all things are become new.
> And all things are of God, who hath reconciled us to himself by Jesus Christ, and hath given to us the ministry of reconciliation. (2 Corinthians 5:17–18)

Before I accepted what Jesus Christ did by acknowledging Him as my Lord and Savior, I was just Olubukola Oluwasanya, the son of my earthly biological father, born in sin. However, the moment I acknowledged Jesus's sacrifice as being for me, I was adopted into the family of God. My spirit was changed from the spirit of sin to the spirit of righteousness. I became a new creature that never existed before, and I—and my name—changed from Olubukola Oluwasanya to Olubukola Oluwasanya-God.

It is only in Christianity that change of parentage is possible.

I should go about and introduce myself to anyone who wants to know me as "Bukola Oluwasanya-God, the adopted son of the Almighty God, bought with the price of God's only Son, Jesus Christ."

That is who we are now. We have acknowledged Jesus Christ as our Lord and Savior. That is your new identity. You are now a son or daughter of God because Jesus is for you.

Jesus Christ is for you, He paid the price for you and He did it for you. He has restored man's position of authority and dominion here on earth. Man is no more subject to the elements of the earth, because Jesus has overcome the world for our sake. He said all authority in heaven and on earth has been given to Him and He in turn has handed it over to us through the use of His name, that at the name of Jesus every knee shall bow. (Philippians 2:10–11)

CHAPTER 5

In Him

And we know that the Son of God is come,
and hath given us an understanding, that
we may know him that is true, and we are in
him that is true, even in his Son Jesus Christ.
This is the true God, and eternal life.

—1 John 5:20

Our adoption is not just changing our names. It is a grafting into Christ. I can recall my ordinary-level biology teacher discussing grafting. She said, "This is an embedding of a plant's shoot into another plant, and the main plant now supplies nutrients for the grafted shoot. Normally, grafting is of a weak plant being put into a strong, well-established plant."

In the same manner, we have been embedded into Christ. The life we now live is not the same as the life of sin we were born with.

I am crucified with Christ: nevertheless I live; yet not I, but Christ liveth in me: and the life which I now live in the flesh I live by the faith of the Son of God, who loved me, and gave himself for me. (Galatians 2:20)

When God wanted to rescue us, He gave us the Law. However, the Law was not able to achieve that purpose because it became a stumbling block. God had to pay the ultimate price by sending His Son to die for our sin. By the death of Christ, we can also be dead to the Law and sin. The real good news is that Christ did not just die and it ended there. He arose, and He is alive so that we can also live with Him by faith that His sacrifice was for us.

Romans 6 clearly lays this out for our understanding. Many as have chosen to accept the redemptive work of Christ and have been baptized into Him—and invariably baptized into His death. Therefore, we have also become dead to the sin that ruled over us through the blunder of Adam in the garden of Eden. He had an identity crisis and wanted to be like God when he was actually created like God in the first place.

Since we were baptized into His death, we are also raised with Him in His resurrection. Our death to sin frees us from the effects and influences of sin that reigned in our lives before the coming of Christ. Sin had turned us into slaves. We were disobeying the dictates and ways of God as He had intended from the beginning. Thanks be to God that He sent

His Son to die in our place and pay the price for our sinful nature.

In the same way, the resurrection of Christ—and us being raised with Him—signifies us overcoming the power of sin and death in our lives. Sin has no more influence over us, and we are not to obey its persuasions to disobey God.

We know that we are in Christ because He has given us His spirit, and that as He is, so are we in this world (1 John 4:13–17).

If that is the case, our lives should possess the same characteristics of Jesus Christ when He was here of earth.

Let us just take a look at some characteristics exhibited by Christ when He was here on earth:

Sinless

> For we have not an high priest which cannot be touched with the feeling of our infirmities; but was in all points tempted like as we are, yet without sin. (Hebrews 4:15)

When Jesus Christ was on earth, He was tempted in all things and in every way, yet He did not sin.

We have the same ability to overcome the lures of sin because we are made like Him on earth. That is why Paul says that sin cannot have dominion over us because we are no longer under the Law, but under grace (Romans 6:14).

Supernatural Knowledge

Jesus exhibited His ability of knowledge. He was conversant with the Word of God, and He had knowledge in knowing about things.

Knowledge of the Word

At the tender age of twelve, Jesus was already having high-level discussions with the elders. The Pharisees were amazed at his insights (Luke 2:46–47).

Those of us who are now in Christ are to exhibit the same trait because it enabled Jesus to resist the devil's temptation after his fast in the wilderness. It will help us resist the devil in our own lives too. That is why Paul admonished Timothy and us to study to show ourselves approved of God so that we will not be messed up and put to shame, rightly unscrambling the Word of God (2 Timothy 2:15).

Knowledge of Other things

In a classic show of superiority, Jesus outclassed the tax collectors and individuals who were looking for crimes to accuse Him of.

> He instructed Peter to go fishing and he will find money enough for His tax and Peter's. Jesus knew when the fish will be there and where the money will be. (Matthew 17:27)

On many occasions, the Bible records that Jesus knew what was in the mind of His adversaries and His disciples. This sort of knowledge is also available to us because those of us who have accepted Christ have been given His Spirit. He will teach us all things and reveal all things to us (John 14).

Power

Jesus had the power to heal, forgive, and deliver. He healed the sick, delivered the oppressed, and forgave sins.

> How God anointed Jesus of Nazareth with the Holy Ghost and with power: who went about doing good, and healing all that were oppressed of the devil; for God was with him. (Acts 10:38)

This same power is available to us; Jesus Christ Himself said it and added that we will even do greater works than what he had done, when he walked on earth:

> Verily, verily, I say unto you, He that believeth on me, the works that I do shall he do also; and greater works than these shall he do; because I go unto my Father. (John 14:12)

Authority

Jesus had and worked in great authority when He was here on earth. There are several accounts that give credence to this, such as commanding demonic powers to free their captives, but the most profound was commanding the winds and the turbulent waves of the sea to be still.

> And the same day, when the even was come, he saith unto them, Let us pass over unto the other side.
> And when they had sent away the multitude, they took him even as he was in the ship. And there were also with him other little ships.
> And there arose a great storm of wind, and the waves beat into the ship, so that it was now full.
> And he was in the hinder part of the ship, asleep on a pillow: and they awake him, and say unto him, Master, carest thou not that we perish?
> And he arose, and rebuked the wind, and said unto the sea, Peace, be still. And the wind ceased, and there was a great calm. (Mark 4:35–41)

This same authority has been given on to us who believe.

> Jesus said if we have faith, we will tell a mountain to relocate its position from one place to another, all that is required of us is to only believe and we shall have what we desire. (Mark 11:23–24)

Eternal Life

The fact that Jesus rose from the dead and is no longer in the grave is evidence that He lives eternally. This was the only thing we didn't have in the garden of Eden since God drove

Adam and Eve out of the garden of Eden before they got to take of the tree of life and live forever:

> And the Lord God said, Behold, the man is become as one of us, to know good and evil: and now, lest he put forth his hand, and take also of the tree of life, and eat, and live forever:
> Therefore the Lord God sent him forth from the garden of Eden, to till the ground from whence he was taken.
> So he drove out the man; and he placed at the east of the garden of Eden Cherubims, and a flaming sword which turned every way, to keep the way of the tree of life. (Genesis 3:22–24)

In John 3:16: God finally gave this to us through the price He paid by Jesus's death on the cross for us. We can now live eternally like Christ and with Christ.

These are the same characteristics that humans lost due to the fall in the garden of Eden. Jesus has handed all of them back to us. Our identities have been restored, and much more has been given to us.

People in the Bible have exhibited some of these restored characteristics. We can draw examples from them and emulate them. The Bible says we should follow those who obtained the promise through faith and patience (Hebrews 6:12).

CHAPTER 6

Just Like

Elias was a man subject to like passions as
we are, and he prayed earnestly that it might
not rain: and it rained not on the earth by
the space of three years and six months.
And he prayed again, and the heaven gave
rain, and the earth brought forth her fruit.
—James 5:17–18

There is nothing written about believers in the Bible that is not practicable. A friend of mine calls the Bible "the user manual of man and life." It chronicles the four critical questions of life: the what, when, why, and how questions.

What is man? When was man created? Why was man created? How is man to function? The characteristics of Jesus give us answers to these questions, and many people have exhibited these characteristics.

Elijah as referred to as a prophet in the book of James,

but he was a man like you and me. He was under the Law (Old Covenant) and not under the adoption (New Covenant) like we who have come to accept Jesus Christ. The accounts of his life on earth show that he exhibited virtually all the characteristics of Christ that we looked at in the last chapter. We can review several other people's lives to see how practicable the new life is that God gives us through Jesus Christ.

We are going to look at Elijah's protégée, Elisha. Many people think Elijah was a special one. They see him as one in a million and think that God just wanted to use him as a special example. It only happens once in many generation. He was taken from earth in a chariot of fire, but he did not die. Enoch also walked with God and was said to be no more because God took him.

Elisha was the servant or student of Elijah, and he asked for a double portion of Elijah's anointing. Jesus told His believers that we will do greater works than He had done on earth. Reviewing Elisha's life and that of Elijah, Elisha actually performed twice as many miracles in his life than Elijah did.

The most profound was that, at the time Elisha died, only one person had been raised from the dead through Him, but it did not end there. God (the Master Architect) worked all things together for good and the glory of His name.

The story was recorded of some young men who were

going to bury a friend who had died, but because they were afraid of approaching Moabite warriors, they quickly threw the young man's body into Elisha's grave. When the dead body touched Elisha's bones, the young man came to life and stood on his feet (2 Kings 13:20–21).

Let us take a look at this man's life vis-à-vis the characteristics of Christ that we said we are to exhibit as the adopted sons and daughters of God.

Sinless

There was no account of the prophet doing anything contrary to the instructions of God. Even when Elisha felt threatened, he did not flinch—unlike his predecessor who asked God to kill him because he thought he was the only righteous person left in Israel.

Supernatural Knowledge

God bestowed supernatural knowledge on Elisha so that he was able to know the discussion going on in the bedroom of the king of Syria with regard to his war strategy against Israel. Elisha revealed it to the king of Israel, and they were saved from the ambush (2 Kings 6).

He was also vast in the Word of God. He instructed the king and the children of Israel about the right path to tread to avoid incurring the wrath of God.

Power

He exhibited great powers from the moment he received the mantle from Elijah: repeating the crossing of the Jordan River on dry ground, floating the axe head, and raising of the dead young man through his own dry bones.

There are several examples to include here, but these illustrate the seemingly impossible situation. All things are possible to those who believe and have God as their father (Mark 9:23).

Authority

This area may sound hard to accept, but it is the truth. Believers have the "say" ability because of the authority that we have through Christ. After Elisha received the mantle, some silly young men thought it would be wise to ridicule the prophet, maybe because of the way he was dressed. Some generals had once referred to the servant of Elisha as a "mad fellow" because of how he was dressed (2 Kings 9:11).

The young men were insulting Elisha about his bald head. In response, he used his authority as a man of God to curse them. As a result, two female bears appeared from a bush and killed forty-two of them.

As believers, we have the authority to curse everything that brings us shame and embarrassment. We can curse anything that may be standing in the way of victory. Say to the mountain standing in your way, be removed, and be thrown into the sea (Mark 11:23).

Eternal Life

You will agree with me that a man like Elisha joined the great cloud of witnesses (Hebrews 12:1), and they are watching us who believe to emulate and even surpass them in demonstrating the characteristics of Christ here on earth.

Someone may say Elisha is an Old Testament individual, his time is different from ours, and he is not faced with our own kinds of challenges. In his time, God talked to people more on a one-on-one basis. Also, he was a prophet.

These are true, but he was disadvantaged compared to us. We operate in the New Testament, while Elisha operated in the shadow of the glory available to us who believe in this day and age. Looking into the life of a seemingly ordinary individual who believed in the sacrifice of Christ for his own life will show us that we can display the same characteristics of Christ.

The book of Acts records the wonderful experience of the baptism of the Holy Spirit and the addition of more believers to the initial three thousand who were converted on that day. The Bible did not say anything special about this particular individual or record any special event on the day he was converted. Therefore, he was just an individual who heard the Gospel, believed, and received the provision for his life. The only time he was mentioned was when some dedicated and trustworthy individuals were needed to ease the responsibilities of the apostles. He was selected as one of the first deacons of the church. His name is Stephen, and he was said to be full of faith and the Holy Ghost (Acts 6:5).

Stephen lived a short life as a believer, but in that short time, he displayed all the attributes of Christ that were discussed earlier.

Sinless

As soon as Stephen gave his life to Christ by accepting that the sacrifice of Christ was for him, all his sins were forgiven. He became sinless. He continued in his newfound status, and that was why he was chosen to be one of the first seven deacons. The selection criteria required being honest, being full of the Holy Ghost, and demonstrating wisdom (Acts 6:3).

Knowledge

The Bible records that some individuals were arguing with Stephen about the Word of God. They were astonished that they could not gainsay his words because of the level of wisdom with which he spoke, and they had to bear false witnesses against him.

Stephen had just given his life to Christ a few months earlier, but within that short time, he had distinct knowledge of God's Word because he was full of the Holy Spirit—our teacher (John 14:26).

He even gave a chronicle of Christ from Abraham to the high priest and the council.

Power

The Bible specifically recorded concerning Stephen being full of power:

> And Stephen, full of faith and power, did great wonders and miracles among the people. (Acts 6:8)

The Bible documented that he was full of power and did great wonders and miracles.

Authority

As a believer, Stephen was full of faith and the Holy Ghost. He possessed the authority of a believer, and he could use it as Elisha did. Instead of cursing those who were stoning him to death, Stephen prayed for God's mercy upon them because he had judged them as ignorant of the consequences of their actions (Acts 7:60).

Eternal Life

> But he, being full of the Holy Ghost, looked up steadfastly into heaven, and saw the glory of God, and Jesus standing on the right hand of God,

> And said, Behold, I see the heavens opened, and the Son of man standing on the right hand of God.
>
> And they stoned Stephen, calling upon God, and saying, Lord Jesus, receive my spirit.
>
> And he kneeled down, and cried with a loud voice, Lord, lay not this sin to their charge. And when he had said this, he fell asleep. (Acts 7:55–56, 59–60)

Because Stephen spoke courageously about Jesus Christ, Jesus gave him a standing ovation. When Stephen was stoned, he handed his spirit directly to the Lord Jesus and fell asleep. Stephen slept in the Lord, and the Bible tells us that those of us who sleep in the Lord will rise again to be with Him for eternity (1 Thessalonians 4:14–16).

The life we are called to live is practical and attainable. It is not some myth or fairy tale. It is who we are. It is what we were created as. Even when humanity lost it in the garden of Eden, Jesus Christ came and paid the price for our adoption. He translated us into sons and daughters of God. We are joint heirs with Jesus Christ because Christ and we are one and the same.

We are in Christ, and Christ is in us. He is the head, and we are His body:

> For as the body is one, and hath many members, and all the members of that one body, being many, are one body: so also is Christ.
>
> For by one Spirit are we all baptized into one body, whether we be Jews or Gentiles,

whether we be bond or free; and have been all made to drink into one Spirit.

For the body is not one member, but many.

If the foot shall say, Because I am not the hand, I am not of the body; is it therefore not of the body?

And if the ear shall say, Because I am not the eye, I am not of the body; is it therefore not of the body?

If the whole body were an eye, where were the hearing? If the whole were hearing, where were the smelling?

But now hath God set the members every one of them in the body, as it hath pleased him.

And if they were all one member, where were the body?

But now are they many members, yet but one body.

And the eye cannot say unto the hand, I have no need of thee: nor again the head to the feet, I have no need of you.

Nay, much more those members of the body, which seem to be more feeble, are necessary:

And those members of the body, which we think to be less honorable, upon these we bestow more abundant honor; and our uncomely parts have more abundant comeliness.

For our comely parts have no need: but God hath tempered the body together, having given more abundant honor to that part which lacked.

That there should be no schism in the body; but that the members should have the same care one for another.

And whether one member suffer, all the members suffer with it; or one member be honored, all the members rejoice with it.

Now ye are the body of Christ, and members in particular. (1 Corinthians 12:12–27)

Every part of the body is interdependent. Christ depends on us to showcase His mercy, love, and power to the world. We depend on Christ for direction and power since we are just like Him and because we are in Him.

CHAPTER 7

Our Inheritance

> Blessed be the God and Father of our Lord
> Jesus Christ, which according to his abundant
> mercy hath begotten us again unto a lively
> hope by the resurrection of Jesus Christ from
> the dead,
> To an inheritance incorruptible, and undefiled,
> and that fadeth not away, reserved in heaven
> for you, Who are kept by the power of God
> through faith unto salvation ready to be
> revealed in the last time. (1 Peter 1:3–5)

We are begotten to an inheritance, a legacy that cannot be corrupted, cannot be defiled, will not fade away and its forever available to us.

It is our legacy, our birthright as children of God, to behave like our Father and our brother Jesus Christ, since we have accepted Christ as our Lord and the sacrifice he offered on the cross at Calvary and this legacy is not susceptible to ruins.

Jesus Christ told a parable to the disciples which to me succinctly explains the incorruptibility of our inheritance.

> Another parable put he forth unto them, saying, The kingdom of heaven is likened unto a man which sowed good seed in his field:
> But while men slept, his enemy came and sowed tares among the wheat, and went his way.
> But when the blade was sprung up, and brought forth fruit, then appeared the tares also.
> So the servants of the householder came and said unto him, Sir, didst not thou sow good seed in thy field? from whence then hath it tares?
> He said unto them, An enemy hath done this. The servants said unto him, Wilt thou then that we go and gather them up?
> But he said, Nay; lest while ye gather up the tares, ye root up also the wheat with them.
> Let both grow together until the harvest: and in the time of harvest I will say to the reapers, Gather ye together first the tares, and bind them in bundles to burn them: but gather the wheat into my barn.
> Then Jesus sent the multitude away, and went into the house: and his disciples came unto him, saying, Declare unto us the parable of the tares of the field.
> He answered and said unto them, He that soweth the good seed is the Son of man;
> The field is the world; the good seed are the children of the kingdom; but the tares are the children of the wicked one;
> The enemy that sowed them is the devil; the harvest is the end of the world; and the reapers are the angels.
> As therefore the tares are gathered and burned in the fire; so shall it be in the end of this world.

The Son of man shall send forth his angels, and
they shall gather out of his kingdom all things
that offend, and them which do iniquity;
And shall cast them into a furnace of fire:
there shall be wailing and gnashing of teeth.
(Matthew 13:24–30, 36–41)

In this fairly long parable, the Lord Jesus told His disciples about the kingdom of God and the inheritance we stand to gain as bought, adopted, and grafted children of God in Christ.

The owner of a farm was informed that there had been an attempt by the enemy to corrupt and hinder the growth of the wheat he had planted on his farm. Contrary to logic and farming principles—to quickly try to weed out the tares that were planted among the wheat—he told his servants to leave them to grow together. This action of his, as the Lord revealed to me, signifies the following:

Avoidance of Error

The master did not want any errors to occur while the servants were weeding out the tares and thistles. They might mistakenly uproot the wheat in the process because they might not be able to accurately differentiate between the wheat shoots and the tares and thistles at that stage.

In addition, he did not want the wheat to be disturbed or tainted in any way. While the servants were weeding out the tares and thistles, they might disturb the wheat bed. They might even drop soil on some of the younger wheat shoots, which could make it difficult for them to sprout as they were meant to and in their own time. However, when the wheat was ripe to harvest, they could easily differentiate between the two. All the shoots would have germinated at their own time and pace—without any disturbance.

In the same way, God has left us here on earth to grow with the evil and decadence in the world. He wants to make us fully ready for His kingdom in the latter days. He is allowing those who are young in the faith to be tried and tested and make their calling sure.

This is an answer to someone who might be questioning why God would leave us in this world in the midst of iniquities and struggles.

Confident of the Quality of the Seed

The master was very confident about the quality of the wheat seeds he planted on his farm. He was confident that the tares and thistles would not harm the wheat in any way, which was contrary to the expectation of the evil one who planted the tares and thistles.

God is so confident of the seeds that we are because we are grafted in Christ. Being born again is not of corruptible seed, but the incorruptible seed of the Word of God is alive and abides forever (1 Peter 1:23). The Word of God (John 1) that brought about a rebirth for us is living and can bear under any circumstance or situation.

God was confident enough to say, "Let both grow together

until harvest." His Word in our hearts brought us into His family and can stand any opposition. We will emerge victorious, like the wheat that grew healthy and was not affected in a negative way by the tares and thistles.

Children of God bought by the blood of sacrifice, stand firm. Stand your ground against whatever opposition may arise or has arisen because of your faith and belief in God as your Father.

The Word of God that you believed—that brought you into the kingdom of God—is in your heart and your being, and it can never be corrupted. It can never be stained. It will never fade, and it will always stand. That is our inheritance in Christ.

God is confident in you.

CHAPTER 8

Manifest

For the earnest expectation of the creature
waiteth for the manifestation of the sons of God.
—Romans 8:19

We can shout, "Hallelujah!" We can rejoice and be glad. All that we lost by the sin of Adam—due to his lack of a clear understanding of his true identity in the garden of Eden—we have regained by faith in Jesus Christ and the His sacrifice on the cross of Calvary. Because our sins have been paid for and we have been adopted as sons of God, we have an inheritance that cannot be corrupted, dishonored, faded, or taken away.

Now that our dominion is restored, our authority is reestablished. Pure knowledge is available to us. Is that all? Is that where it ends? No!

When God created us, He gave us the responsibilities to

be fruitful, to multiply, to replenish the earth, and to subdue it: to have dominion over the fish of the sea, over the fowl of the air, over every living thing that moves upon the earth (Genesis 1:28). Therefore, when Adam and Eve fell to the deception of the serpent (Satan), humankind lost the ability to carry out these responsibilities.

When Christ paid the debt for our sins, it restored us back to God and his position. We are liable for carrying out these twofold responsibilities of fruitfulness and dominion.

How are we expected to do this? What it is significance? Children are being born on earth every minute of the day—and the world is already going into ruin.

That is the real essence of all we have been sharing in this book. God wants us to understand our identity on earth at this time. Many of us children of God are quick to acknowledge that we are not of this world—even though we are in it. The essence of that difference is that we are expected to affect the world. That is why we are in it.

God is confident in the seed He planted in the world. That is why He is keeping us here. At the time of harvest, the wheat will stand in all its golden glory, with a backdrop of the sun, and the thistles will be green, looking out of place in the field. The wheat will stand undeterred and ready to be harvested—contrary to what we find on earth these days.

The world is influencing the children of the kingdom, and they have almost literally taken over the church. Some churches have become nightclubs in the name of "being a Jew to win the Jews and a Gentile to win the Gentiles" (1

Corinthians 9:20). The church has embraced homosexuality to the point of allowing same-sex marriage, ordaining self-confessed homosexuals to conduct Holy Ordinances of God, and having homosexual congregations in the name of a church.

Even though these things were not as prominent in the days of the apostle Paul, the Holy Spirit inspired him to give us a glimpse of our purpose on earth. God is keeping us here. He could have just taken us up to be with Him at the very moment we accepted His gift of salvation through Jesus Christ.

Paul explained that it was not only humans that were in bondage due to the sin of Adam. All of creation has been groaning since then, awaiting deliverance, which can only come through the manifestation of the sons and daughters of God (Romans 8).

One of the consequences of Adam's sin was that man would henceforth find it difficult to till the ground to get good harvest from it. That was not how God ordained for the ground to be from the beginning. The ground was supposed to be fruitful, was it not the same earth that God commanded to "bring forth living creature after his kind, cattle, and creeping things, and beast of the earth, which it did, and God adjudged it as being good" (Genesis 1:24–25). However, for the sin of Adam, the earth became a producer of thorns and thistles.

We are the sons and daughters of God, and the whole of creation is waiting for our manifestation so that the world can be delivered from the consequences of sin and function in the way and manner God created them from the start.

How are we to do this? What does it mean for the children of God to manifest? We shall look at this under the three characteristics that we identify as man's identity that he failed to understand in the garden of Eden and eventually lost: God's image, dominion, and knowledge.

Manifesting God's Image

What is God's image? God tell us who He is and what he represents. That is why we are here and can claim redemption. God is love (1 John 4:8). God gave His Son to pay the price for our sins because He loved the world so much (John 3:16).

Therefore, for us to manifest the image of God to our world, we are to work in love. Jesus corroborated this statement when He said,

> "A new commandment I give unto you, that ye love one another; as I have loved you, that ye also love one another. By this shall all men know that ye are my disciples, if ye have love one to another." (John 13:34–35)

It is the love of God, that we should exhibit towards one another in the Kingdom, which identifies us as children of God. Apostle Paul added his voice by encouraging us with this command: "Be ye therefore followers of God, as dear children; and walk in love, as Christ also hath loved us, and hath given himself for us an offering and a sacrifice to God for a sweet-smelling savour. (Ephesians 5:1–2)

But what do we have right now in the church? Strife, schism, and self—not love.

The church of today has the two extremes of human social status: the richest and the poorest. The rich believe their wealth is the blessing of God, but it is meant for only them and their immediate families. That is not the way the Church of Christ started. All believers had all things in common; no special bounty for a select few and those that had more possessions sold them, so that every man's needs are met (Acts 2:44–45).

This particular point came to me more vividly at a recent birthday celebration of an older friend. The minister was telling us that our lives were meant to be lived serving God, helping humanity, and taking care of ourselves. On the point of serving others, he affirmed that we all need to survive on earth. God has made a provision that is to be supplied by us and for us. He stated that children are made to go into child labor because their biological parents cannot afford to send them to school. That is not part of God's plan for these children, especially those whose parents are believers. It is expected that those who have the financial means were meant to make it available so that everyone can have all things in common—and everyone can have their needs met.

So, my brothers and sisters, how are you manifesting the image of God (love) as children of God. If you can speak in tongues, prophesy, move mountains, and even give all that you have, but yet do not love your neighbor, all that is worthless (1 Corinthians 13).

It is not just in the giving. It is in the motive, attitude, and understanding that you are representing God to the world, thereby drawing others to God. Invariably, you are fulfilling the first responsibility of being fruitful, multiplying, and replenishing the earth according to your kind because love begets love.

Manifesting Dominion

Dominion is taking charge, control, or authority.

How are we to manifest control and authority in the world and fulfill our primary responsibilities on earth? Is it by being in the seat of government and controlling a nation and her people? Is it having power to live the way we want? Is it having the authority to cast out demons?

None of these are what God expects of us.

I love the biblical story of a boy born to a family after the mother had difficulty during her pregnancy and birth. She decided to put the poor boy in bondage—just as humankind and the whole of creation were put into the bondage of sin because of Adam and Eve's indiscretion.

This boy was named Jabez (distress) by the mother because of the difficult delivery, and his name became a stumbling block until he grew up (1 Chronicles 4:9). The young man did not stop there; he sought God in prayer asking for help:

> And Jabez called on the God of Israel, saying, Oh that thou wouldest bless me indeed, and enlarge my coast, and that thine hand might be with me, and that thou wouldest keep me from evil, that it may not grieve me! And God granted him that which he requested. (1 Chronicles 4:10)

The Lord granted him his request, which is why the passage said he was more honorable (distinguished) than his peers and brethren.

The content of his prayer explains how the sons and daughters of God are meant to manifest dominion in the world we live in.

Bless Me!

When you are blessed, your needs are met and you are a channel of blessing. That gives you the ability to influence others by providing for them and directing them in the ways of God. He who pays the pipe dictates the tune.

Enlarge My Coast

This is a request to have a large sphere of influence. You cannot compare the impact of a so-called local champion to one with international exposure in any venture or endeavor in life. That person's sphere of influence might not be up to par.

Our desire as children of God is to pray for more grounds for Jesus, more grounds for the kingdom of God on earth, and not allowing the Islamization of nations that is currently taking place under our very noses.

Let Your Hand Be with Me!

People who the hand of God is with will always get help—and they will always be walking in the right direction because the hand of God will always guide and correct them.

People will always follow a visionary individual—either down the right path or the wrong one. As long as people can perceive that they seem to know what they are doing and where they are going, they will follow them.

As children of God, Jesus commissioned us to be fishers of others. The only reason we do not seem to be catching enough fishes for the kingdom is because the fishes don't seem to see us as people who know what we are doing or where we are going. We must stop the constant infighting and denominational breakaways and the continuous strive to emulate the ways of the world.

Keep Me from Evil!

I will use two Yoruba (my native language) adages here:

> If fire is burning you and your child, you will have to put out the fire on you first so that you will be able to properly concentrate on putting out the fire on your child.

If you desire to exhibit dominion, you have to be free from every possible form of bondage. If you are under the bondage of evil, how will you be able to go out and bring deliverance to other individuals and the earth? You need your deliverance first, but many children of God do not understand that they are no longer under any curse because the curse of sin has been broken. We have perfect liberty.

Walk in the light of the freedom you have in Christ—and you will be walking in dominion.

> If someone is going to give clothes to another person, we have to first examine the quality of what he or she is wearing to ascertain that what he or she wants to give is worth taking in the first place.

If a child of God who desires to preach deliverance to anyone is in bondage, what is the attraction for anyone to accept the message of deliverance?

The Bible tells you to let your light shine. Only a light that has not been covered or kept in hiding can shine. Children of God, claim your deliverance, shine your light to the world, and bring them the succor that they have been groaning for.

Manifesting Knowledge

> The fear of the Lord is the beginning of knowledge: but fools despise wisdom and instruction. (Proverbs 1:7)

To fear God is to manifest knowledge, but we do not seem to fear God. We take Him for granted. Too many children of God say, "God understands," "My God is not a hard God," or "God is too merciful to judge you like that or instantly."

They fail to realize that God is our Father. He loves us so much. While we were sinners, He sent His Son to die in our place. He is also a consuming fire!

He is a just God, and He has to uphold justice. Why would he send sinners to hell and allow you—who behaves in the same way and manner of the sinner—to go to heaven because you opened your mouth one day and declared your acceptance of Jesus's sacrifice on the cross for your sins? Did you amend your evil ways? Did you change?

He is a righteous God. He will always do what is right. To manifest that knowledge, you have to realize that your life should emulate that of your Father. Always do what is right—just like Him. Do not cheat, steal, gossip, or be fraudulent.

He is a holy God. He has commanded that His children must be holy unto Him because He is holy.

He is Spirit—so we must worship Him in spirit and in truth.

He is Faithful—so we must believe Him.

He is Love—so we must love Him.

Printed in the United States
By Bookmasters